MAKE ME LA...

REAL CLASSY

SILLY SCHOOL JOKES

by Rick and Ann Walton with John Jansen

pictures by Brian Gable

Carolrhoda Books, Inc. • Minneapolis

Q: Why did the fish go to school?

A: He heard they had bookworms.

Q: Where did the math student eat lunch?

A: At the multiplication table.

Q: What do you get if you're allergic to the letter *B*?

A: B-hives.

Q: Why did the math student bring a ruler to bed?

A: She wanted to see how long she slept.

Q: What's the best way to shoot an L-shaped arrow?

A: With an L-bow.

Q: Where did the student write his poems?

A: Under the poet-tree.

Q: Why did the student bring his glasses home?

A: To study for the eye test.

Q: Why should you throw an *S* at a cat if you want it to go away?

A: Because it will make the cat SCAT.

Q: What color did the art teacher paint the sun and wind?

A: He painted the sun rose and the wind blue.

Q: Why do *O* and *M* like each other?

A: Because they have so much in COMMON.

Q: Did the teacher write with his left or right hand?

A: Neither. He wrote with a pencil.

Q: How should you feel if a letter *N* gives you a pat on the back?

A: N-couraged.

Q: What letters of the alphabet should you stay away from?

A: *N M E.*

Q: What did the science teachers say was at the center of Earth?

A: The letter *R.*

Q: Why are there so few letter *Q*s in the dictionary?

A: Because *Q* is not in DEMAND.

Q: What did the witch teach in school?

A: Spelling.

Q: What did the letter *T* say to the pencil?

A: "You've crossed me for the last time!"

Q: Where do baby cows eat their school lunches?

A: In the calf-eteria.

Q: Why is the letter *A* at the head of the alphabet?

A: Because it's in CHARGE.

Q: Where do you eat lunch if you have a cold?

A: In the cough-eteria.

Q: Why did the alligator do well in school?

A: He always gave snappy answers.

Q: Why did the teacher need glasses?

A: She had bad pupils.

Q: What letter is always in hot water?

A: *T.*

Q: What did the school janitor say when the kids asked him about his job?

A: "It's picking up."

Q: Why was the chess team in the dark?

A: They lost all their matches.

Q: Why did the teacher wear sunglasses?

A: Her students were very bright.

Q: What is the capital of France?

A: The letter *F.*

Q: What's the best way to catch a school of fish?

A: With bookworms.

Q: When did the American patriots celebrate a letter?

A: At the Boston *T* Party.

Q: Why were there only twenty-four letters in the alphabet two hundred years ago?

A: Because U and I weren't there.

Q: How do we know Hamlet had trouble spelling rabbit?

A: Because he asked himself, "Two *B*s or not two *B*s."

Q: How do scholars get across the sea?

A: They use scholarships.

Q: What should you feed the letter *C*?

A: C-food.

Q: What's black when it's clean and white when it's dirty?

A: A chalkboard.

MLE: "How did you feel when you got a D on your test?"

KT: "D-graded!"

Q: Where did the teacher grow her vegetables?

A: In the kinder-garden.

Q: Why did the students wear sunglasses?

A: It was an illuminating lesson.

Q: What two letters are all right?

A: OK.

Q: Why did the report card sting?

A: It was all Bs.

Q: How would you feel if you ate a lot of *P*s?

A: *P*s-full.

Q: Why does the letter *Z* frequently get lost?

A: Because it's always in a HAZE.

Q: What did the student have just before he got his report card?

A: Grade Expectations.

Q: What did the teacher say when the student wrote *WETHR*?

A: "That's the worst spell of weather we've seen in a long time."

Q: What do you find twice as much of in nighttime as in daytime?

A: The letter *T*.

Q: Which letter is magical?

A: The Fair-E.

Q: Was the student in a bad mood during finals?

A: No, he was just a little testy.

Q: Why did the student give his report card a parachute?

A: Because all his grades were falling.

Q: Why did the naughty student hang around school?

A: Because he was suspended.

Q: What happened when the *J* suddenly came onto the baseball field?

A: It made the ump JUMP.

Q: Why will the letter *A* send food into space?

A: Because it will make your lunch LAUNCH.

Q: Why don't spies like the letter *S*?

A: Because it makes their lip SLIP.

Q: How did the writer get across the water?

A: She took the penmanship.

Q: What did the astronomy student get for taking second place?

A: The constellation prize.

Q: Why should you never eat a treat that has the letter *H* on it?

A: Because it makes the treat a THREAT.

Q: Why is an *E* a welcome sight to a hungry person?

A: Because it turns a fast into a FEAST.

Q: Why did the student hate learning about Egypt?

A: She was in denial.

Q: How do you feel if a giant letter *D* sits on you?

A: D-pressed.

Q: What did the science teacher say when she was asked, "Which is faster, heat or cold?"

A: She said "Heat, because you can catch cold."

Q: Why was the geometry teacher so confusing?

A: Because he talked in circles.

Q: Why was the math student afraid of the number 7?

A: Because 7 8 9.

Q: Why did the teacher go to the beach?

A: He wanted to test the waters.

Q: Who haunts the school?

A: The school spirit.

Q: Why should you take an *R* away from Fred if he's hungry?

A: Because it gets Fred FED.

Q: Why should you give the letter *R* to a fiend?

A: Because it will make the fiend a FRIEND.

Q: Why should you never put an *S* on a lime?

A: Because it makes the lime SLIME.

Q: What did the vampire learn in school?

A: Punctur-ation.

Q: Why do uncles and aunts like to take the letter *E* away from a naughty niece?

A: Because they know that it will make their niece NICE.

Q: Why did the skeleton skip school?

A: It didn't have the guts for it.

Q: Why did Dracula go to school?

A: He was looking for the alpha-bat.

Q: Why are the letters *T* and *E* so popular?

A: Because they're always in STYLE and never out of DATE.

Q: Where did the ghost go to learn?

A: High ghoul.

Q: Why did the girl break her leg before the school play?

A: She wanted to be in the cast.

Q: Why did the science teacher bring a chicken to school?

A: Her class was doing eggs-periments.

Q: Why are *L* and *I* so straight?

A: Because everyone keeps them in LINE.

Q: Why does Nat's mother like the letter *E*?

A: Because it makes Nat NEAT.

Q: What happens when Ben gets hit by a letter *T*?

A: Ben becomes BENT.

Q: What do you get if someone hits you with a letter *I*?

A: An I-sore.

Q: What do you get when you cross a professor and a monster?

A: The Teacher from the Black Lagoon.

Q: What letter reminds you of looking in the mirror?

A: *W*.

Q: Why is the letter *S* easy to recognize?

A: Because it appears everywhere in PERSON.

Q: Why was it smooth sailing with the report card?

A: It was nothing but straight Cs.

Q: How do you feel if the letter *N* puts a curse on you?

A: N-chanted.

Q: When is a report card like a sheep?

A: When the grades are B-A-A-B-A-A.

Q: Why couldn't the bookworm sneeze?

A: He had his nose in a book.

Q: Why are the letters *L* and *O* so close?

A: Because they're in LOVE.

Q: Who scared the students in the hall?

A: The Lockerness monster.

Q: What book is a good listener?

A: The school 'earbook.

Q: Why should a kid never carry the letter *S* while he's walking on ice?

A: Because it'll make the kid SKID.

Q: Why was the math book so sad?

A: It was full of problems.

Q: Why will the letter *C* never go straight?

A: Because it goes in CIRCLES.

Q: Why was the student afraid to go to school?

A: She didn't want to get stung by the spelling bee.

Q: How did the spelling bee champion correct the word "Beee?"

A: She used an eraser.

Q: What do you get when you cross the letter *M* with the king of cats?

A: The M-purr-er.

Q: Why should you never get in a plane with a letter *T*?

A: Because it will turn the plane into a PLANET.

Q: Why did the school add another floor of English classes?

A: They wanted another story.

Q: How did the music teacher want his students to play?

A: Solo. Solo they couldn't be heard.

Q: Why can the letter *T* run forever?

A: Because it's always in CONDITION and never out of BREATH.

Q: Why was the teacher unpopular?

A: He had no class.

Q: What are there four of in every engine but never found in any car?

A: The letter *E*.

Q: If you want to see a lot of letter *D*s, what should you do?

A: Take a D-tour.

Q: Why did the king go to school?

A: He heard they needed a ruler.

Q: What letter will give you a lift?

A: The L-evator.

Q: Why is an extra *A* a nice thing for someone to have?

A: It turns any place into a PALACE.

Q: What letter likes to swing?

A: The chimpan-Z.

Q: What letter is a game for birds?

A: Crow-K.

Q: How boring was the teacher?

A: He even made the chalk bored.

Q: What was the teacher's favorite dessert?
A: Edu-cake.

Q: What's the best way to shine the letter *B*?
A: With *B*s-wax.

Q: What letter is difficult to figure out?
A: Mister-E.

Q: Why did the dogs go to school?

A: They heard there was going to be a pup rally.

Q: Why should you always carry a *W* with you if you're in a hurry?

A: Because it will make your heels WHEELS.

Q: What do you get if you plant a letter *C*?

A: C-weed.

Q: What three letters do athletes like?

A: *N R G.*

Q: Why was the best-liked teacher also the coolest?

A: Because she had lots of fans.

Q: Where do teachers send students who don't tell the truth?

A: To the lie-brary.

Q: Why are the letters *B* and *D* like a beach?

A: Because they're found next to the C.

Q: How happy was everybody when school finally ended?

A: Even the hands on the clocks applauded.

Q: What letters perform in the circus?

A: The trap-Es.

Q: Why is the letter *V* never late?

A: Because it always shows up in ADVANCE.

Q: Where does the letter *C* go swimming?

A: At the C-shore.

Q: What do you need for music class?

A: A notebook.

Q: How did the gym teacher travel?

A: She went coach.

Q: Who was the best athlete in school?

A: Jim Class.

Q: What do beginning fishers have to learn?

A: Their alpha-bait.

Q: Why was the report card all wet?

A: All the grades were below C level.

Q: What can you always find in the middle of the night?

A: The letter *G*.

Q: Why can't you whisper in school?

A: Because it isn't aloud.

Q: Why doesn't the letter *H* get any visitors?

A: Because it's in the middle of NOWHERE.

Q: What will we see at the end of time?

A: The letter *E*.

Q: Why did the classroom stink?

A: It was full of pew-pils.

Q: What's the difference between an angler and a bad student?

A: One baits his hooks, the other hates his books.

Q: What should you do if you accidentally drop your letter *C* down a well?

A: Go deep-C fishing.

Q: What's bacteria?

A: The rear entrance to the cafeteria.

GG: "How did you feel when you stuck the *D* in the lamp?"

DD: "D-lighted!"

Q: Why is it easy to see the letter *E*?

A: Because it's at the end of your NOSE.

Q: What do beginning gamblers have to learn?

A: Their alphabet.

Q: Why is the letter *L* healthy?

A: Because all's well that ends WELL.

This book is available in two editions:
Library binding by Carolrhoda Books, Inc.,
  a division of Lerner Publishing Group
Soft cover by First Avenue Editions,
  an imprint of Lerner Publishing Group
241 First Avenue North
Minneapolis, MN 55401 U.S.A.

Website address: www.carolrhodabooks.com

Library of Congress Cataloging-in-Publication Data

Walton, Rick.
    Real classy : silly school jokes / by Rick and Ann Walton with John Jansen ;
pictures by Brian Gable.
       p.   cm. — (Make me laugh)
    Summary: A collection of jokes about school and education.
    ISBN: 1–57505–665–8 (lib. bdg. : alk. paper)
    ISBN: 1–57505–740–9 (pbk. : alk. paper)
    1. Schools—Juvenile humor. 2. Education—Juvenile humor. [1. Jokes. 2.
Riddles. 3. Schools—Humor.] I. Walton, Ann, 1963– II. Jansen, John, 1956–
III. Gable, Brian, 1949– ill. IV. Title. V. Series.
PN6231.S3W33 2005
818'.5402—dc22   2003019355

Manufactured in the United States of America
1 2 3 4 5 6 – DP – 10 09 08 07 06 05